973.917 WHI
Whitman, Sylvia,
V is for victory : ><rld War II
SPEEDWAY P.L. 91042244

3 5550 99055381 3

P9-DHM-951

SPEED...
SPEEDWAY, INDIANA

973.917
Whi      Whitman, Sylvia

         V is for victory

            060190

DUE DATE

| | | | |
|---|---|---|---|
| | | | |
| | | | |
| | | | |
| | | | |
| | | | |
| | | | |
| | | | |
| | | | |
| | | | |
| | | | |
| | | | |

WITHDRAWN
Speedway Public Library

SPEEDWAY PUBLIC LIBRARY
SPEEDWAY, INDIANA

1/94

# V
# IS FOR
# VICTORY

SPEEDWAY PUBLIC LIBRARY
SPEEDWAY, INDIANA

# V
# IS FOR
# VICTORY

## THE AMERICAN HOME FRONT DURING WORLD WAR II

Sylvia Whitman

SPEEDWAY PUBLIC LIBRARY
SPEEDWAY, INDIANA

Lerner Publications Company • Minneapolis

*To my parents, for a childhood full of talk and books, and to my husband, Mohamed, for a life full of possibilities and couscous*

The following people also deserve special thanks for their help: BettyLou and Bill Folley, Herman and Christine Kramer, Lee Saunders, Sylvia Choate and Sandy Whitman—who shared their memories and stories on tape; editor Margaret Goldstein—who shepherded an idea from a letter to a book; and the staff of the Orange County Public Library in Orlando.

Copyright © 1993 by Lerner Publications Company

All rights reserved. International copyright secured. No part of this book may be reproduced or transmitted in any form or by any means, electronic or mechanical, including photocopying and recording, or by any information storage or retrieval system, without permission in writing from the publisher, except for the inclusion of brief quotations in an acknowledged review.

LIBRARY OF CONGRESS CATALOGING-IN-PUBLICATION DATA

Whitman, Sylvia, 1961-
    V is for victory : the American home front during World War II /
by Sylvia Whitman.
        p.   cm.
    Includes bibliographical references and index.
    Summary: Describes life in the United States during World War II, discussing such activities as civil defense, the Japanese relocation, rationing, propaganda, and censorship.
    ISBN 0-8225-1727-2
    1. United States—History—1933-1945—Juvenile literature.
2. World War, 1939-1945—United States—Juvenile literature.
[1. World War, 1939-1945—United States.]  I. Title.
E806.W4564   1993
973.917—dc20                                          91-42244
                                                       CIP
                                                       AC

060190

Manufactured in the United States of America

1  2  3   4   5   6   98   97   96   95   94   93

# *Contents*

# BOMBS BRING WAR HOME

*No matter how long it may take us to overcome this premeditated invasion, the American people in their righteous might will win through to absolute victory.*

—President Franklin D.
Roosevelt, December 8, 1941

On December 7, 1941, the United States was taking a day off. All across the country, people were going to church, listening to the radio, or following the adventures of Popeye and Olive Oyl in the "funny pages" of the Sunday paper. In the nation's chilly capital, thousands gathered to watch the Washington Redskins play football against the Philadelphia Eagles. At Pearl Harbor, Hawaii, the base of the American Pacific Fleet, most sailors aboard the ships were sleeping late.

Not everyone was enjoying the Sunday holiday, though. A little after 7:00 A.M., a private in the Army Signal Corps was monitoring radar equipment on the Hawaiian island of Oahu when the screen registered incoming aircraft. He notified his supervisor, who told the soldier not to worry about the signals. Nearby Hickam Field was expecting a flight of planes from California.

In 1941 much of the world was at war, but not the United States. Led by dictator Adolf Hitler, Germany had invaded Poland in 1939. Sticking up for their Polish ally, Britain and France then declared war on Germany—but could not stop its powerful army from occupying most of Europe. Hitler and members of his National Socialist (Nazi) party called themselves a "master race." They wanted to rule the continent, killing or enslaving people they considered "undesirable," such as Jews.

In Asia, Japan was also extending its empire by force, seizing parts of China and other nations. In September 1940, Germany, Italy, and Japan—known as the Axis—formed a military alliance. Although the U.S. government was speaking out against Japanese attacks on China and was supplying Britain with food and weapons to fight Germany, many Americans hoped their country would remain neutral.

Yet, on that morning of December 7, at 7:49 A.M., more than 180 Japanese aircraft zoomed in over Pearl Harbor and began raining bombs on Battleship Row, where dozens of warships sat at anchor, and other military

*The Japanese attack cripples Pearl Harbor.*

*The battleship* Arizona *sinks in flames. More than 1,000 servicemen died when the* Arizona *went down.*

targets. Many residents who heard the explosions assumed the U.S. military was just conducting a drill. After lots of pestering by her five-year-old son, naval wife Hazel Brock looked out the window—and saw an air force barracks blow up. She ran outside, stunned by waves of Japanese bombers flying so low that she could see the pilots' faces.

A second raid followed an hour later. Although the unprepared Americans scrambled to mount a defense with antiaircraft guns, the Japanese inflicted terrible damage. The attack wiped out 188 U.S. aircraft on the ground and destroyed or disabled 19 naval vessels, including five giant battleships.

When the radio announced that all Pearl Harbor workers should report to the base, John Garcia, a 16-year-old pipe fitter apprentice, rode to the docks on his motorcycle. "It was a mess," he recalled in Studs Terkel's *"The Good War": An Oral History of World War Two.* One of the officers asked Garcia to help rescue seamen blasted from the decks. "I brought out I don't know how many bodies and how many were alive and how many dead," Garcia said. "Another man would put them into ambulances and they'd be gone."

It would take weeks to recover the living and the dead, many of them trapped in the steel hulls of capsized ships. All told, the attack killed more than 2,300 servicemen and about 70 civilians. John Garcia's girlfriend died when an American shell fired in defense accidentally fell on her house. At least 1,100 people were wounded. When doctors on Oahu put out an urgent call for blood, 500 donors showed up within an hour. When the staff ran out of containers, they sterilized and filled Coca-Cola bottles.

First by telephone, then by radio, the awful news flashed back across the United States. Many music lovers heard about the attack as they tuned in to CBS Radio for an afternoon concert by the New York Philharmonic orchestra. At pro football games, officials announced that servicemen in the crowd should report to their bases.

"It was a complete shock," remembers BettyLou Folley, a young secretarial school graduate living in suburban New Jersey in 1941. "Everybody was talking about it. It was on the radio all day."

In 1939, a Gallup Poll reported that 58 percent of all Americans believed the United States would be drawn into war. In 1940, Congress had passed the country's first peacetime draft, a system for choosing young men to serve in the military. Americans listened in horror to their radios that year. Broadcasting live from London, reporter Edward R. Murrow described the scene as German bombers ravaged the city. Yet few people expected that the conflict would cross the oceans to U.S. borders.

"You know, we always thought we were invincible; nobody was going to attack us," says Herman Kramer, then a defense worker in Baltimore. "It shocked everybody."

*These photographs of New York City's Times Square—before (top) and after an air raid drill—were taken just five minutes apart. After the siren sounded, pedestrians quickly took cover inside buildings and subways.*

## A CIVILIAN'S WAR

In Washington, President Franklin Delano Roosevelt (FDR) consulted with his advisers. No one knew what was coming next. Was Japan poised to invade the U.S. mainland? Roosevelt put the military on alert and silenced amateur radio operators in case any foreign spies were trying to send radio signals. He ordered extra protection for military bases, bridges, and weapons factories. In case of an attack on the White House, soldiers perched on the roof with machine guns, and a plane at a secret airstrip was ready to whisk the president to safety. Crippled by polio, FDR also carried a gas mask slung over the handles of his wheelchair.

That Sunday evening, while the president held a cabinet meeting, about a thousand Washingtonians sang "The Star-Spangled Banner" and "God Bless America" across from the White House. Unfortunately, the rest of the country did not react so calmly. In Hawaii, the military took charge. It ordered a curfew—everyone off the streets from six at night until six in the morning—and a total blackout. House, street, and building lights were turned off—lest enemy pilots use them to sight a target after dark. John Garcia was driving a truckload of marines into a valley when lights came on inside a house. The soldiers started shooting. The house went dark fast.

Word of the attack spread quickly, missing only the most remote rural areas, and then for only a day or so. All over the nation, Americans looked to the sky, listening for the drone of enemy airplanes. Citrus center Orlando, Florida, fearing an attack on its airport, had a fake grove of orange trees painted on the runways. In Georgia, prison inmates were assigned to defend the coast on round-the-clock shifts. Midwesterners sized up caves and mine shafts as possible bomb shelters. Many cities rigged searchlights and guns on rooftops.

Fear gripped the West Coast, the most likely place for a Japanese invasion of the mainland. In Los Angeles, sirens wailed. Antiaircraft gunners fired at random, injuring several people. In downtown San Francisco, crowds tried to enforce a blackout by stoning and smashing movie marquees and streetcar lights. On the Golden Gate Bridge, all cars had to stop for inspection at a security checkpoint, and a skittish

National Guardsman shot and seriously wounded a woman who didn't brake fast enough.

On December 8, nearly 60 million Americans listened in by radio as the president addressed a joint session of Congress. "Yesterday, December 7, 1941—a date which will live in infamy—the United States of America was suddenly and deliberately attacked by naval and air forces of the empire of Japan," FDR said. He added that the Japanese had also launched offensives against U.S. and British troops stationed in the Pacific, striking Hong Kong, Guam, the Philippines, Wake Island, and Midway. When the president asked for a declaration of war against Japan, only one lawmaker—Republican Jeannette Rankin from Montana, a pacifist—voted "nay."

Few U.S. citizens shared Rankin's belief that the conflict could be resolved peacefully. Lee Saunders, then a young businessman in New York City, remembers:

> There was, of course, a great rush, both that day and in the ensuing days, of young men wanting to enlist. Everybody was very patriotic, and all the fellas wanted to get in on it, because this was not a political situation, this was a case of our country being attacked. . . . We wanted to defend our people.

All sorts of citizens volunteered to defend their communities. The American Legion of Wisconsin tried to organize a militia of deer hunters, and farmers on a Washington state island patrolled the beach with pitchforks. In time, these confused efforts gave way to programs organized by the federal Office of Civilian Defense (OCD). Fiorello H. La Guardia, mayor of New York City and director of the OCD, challenged Americans to give "an hour a day for the U.S.A." In Philadelphia, for instance, lawyers and cabdrivers alike guarded the city's port, taking eight-hour shifts once every six days.

In the first months after the attack on Pearl Harbor, neighborhood block wardens with white helmets, arm bands, and whistles enforced blackouts or brownouts (partial blackouts). Smokers learned to strike their matches only under streetlights. Even the Great White Way of

*Using a map of New York, civilian defense officials plan the citywide response in case of enemy attack.*

Broadway in New York City went dim at dusk—not only to disorient enemy bombers but also to save energy. For home owners, five-and-dime stores sold "blackout accessories": flashlights, candles, first-aid kits, curtains, and shades.

Many towns prepared for air raids. Plane spotters studied silhouettes of enemy aircraft in order to identify an attack squadron. During drills, civilian defense workers sounded alarms—such as the monstrously loud Victory Siren, which ran on a car engine and could break the eardrums of anyone within 100 feet. Block wardens then hustled passersby under cover. Since few communities had bomb shelters, citizens were told to hide in the basement or under a table at the sound of the siren.

Four days after the Japanese attack on Pearl Harbor, Germany and Italy declared war on the United States. By January 1942, the United

States, Britain, and two dozen other countries—known later as the Allies—had pledged to fight together against the Axis.

Along the Atlantic coast, German submarines, or U-boats, began torpedoing American supply vessels. To keep up morale, the navy downplayed the damage, but coastal residents sometimes saw the burning ships sink offshore. Although the Japanese did not land on the beaches of California as many residents feared, in February 1942, a Japanese submarine shelled an oil refinery in Santa Barbara.

To free up military pilots for combat, 80,000 amateur flyers joined the Civil Air Patrol (CAP). Home from college in early 1942, Sylvia Choate rode as an observer in a two-seat Piper Cub airplane, taking notes about roofs and smokestacks on factories. From these CAP reports, authorities knew which landmarks needed to be disguised. Soon the CAP assumed other jobs, such as delivering blood and towing targets so gunners could practice hitting a moving object.

Civil Air Patrol pilots, mostly men too old for the Army Air Corps, also kept watch along the coast. Since women were not allowed to go on flights over the ocean, Sylvia Choate took a full-time CAP job

*A troop of Civil Air Patrol pilots*

*A government poster praises the work of the CAP flyers.*

sending pilots' reports over a Teletype to Washington, D.C. If a CAP flyer sighted an enemy sub, a military plane then took off to sink it.

## CASUALTIES OF SUSPICION

Immediately after the attack on Pearl Harbor, the Federal Bureau of Investigation made mass arrests of foreigners, including 2,000 Japanese. Mobs smashed store windows in Los Angeles's Little Tokyo and destroyed souvenirs stamped "Made in Japan." Rumors about spies led frightened Americans to suspect that every "Nip"—an insulting name for a person of Japanese ancestry—was an enemy agent.

On the evening of December 7, Peter Ota's father, a Japanese immigrant, was leaving a wedding reception in Los Angeles when FBI agents arrested him with a dozen other guests. For days, Mr. Ota's family had no idea where he was. Finally they found him in jail, wearing a prison uniform instead of his tuxedo. Peter Ota, quoted in *"The Good War,"* remembered his mother's reaction:

*Japanese Americans in San Francisco prepare to leave their homes.*

> The shame and humiliation just broke her down.... Shame
> in her culture is worse than death. Right after that day she
> got very ill and contracted tuberculosis. She had to be sent
> to a sanitarium.... She was there till she passed away.

In time, many Japanese families came to know such sorrow. On February 19, 1942, Roosevelt signed Executive Order 9066, which forced more than 110,000 men, women, and children of Japanese ancestry to abandon their homes and businesses. Many of them were never able to recover their property. Two-thirds of them were American citizens.

They cooperated with the government order, however, moving first to temporary assembly centers (like the stables of the Santa Anita racetrack in California) and then to permanent camps in desolate inland areas of the West. "Be prepared for the Relocation Center, which is a pioneer community," a 1942 government pamphlet warned Japanese Americans. The War Relocation Authority provided food, shelter, clothes, jobs, and schools at the camps. Family members stayed together, but living in barracks and eating in dining halls deprived them of their freedom and their privacy. At the Poston camp in the Arizona desert, so much sand blew up through the floorboards that people had to cover their mouths with handkerchiefs in order to breathe. Later, they planted alfalfa between the makeshift buildings to keep down the dust.

Few Americans questioned the government's right to confine citizens behind barbed wire without evidence of wrongdoing. "We were told that these Japanese were dangerous to the country, that Japan had invaded us," recalls Sylvia Choate.

"Everybody just accepted it," agrees BettyLou Folley. "I thought it was terrible." Unlike most Americans, Folley knew some Japanese families personally. She also knew the sting of being caught in the middle. Her own father, an engineer, had emigrated from Germany. He worried about his German relatives overseas as well as his two sons serving in the U.S. military. Some Americans distrusted people of German and Italian descent. "[My father] got some flak from some of the men that worked in the office," Folley recalls. "They would call him 'You Kraut.' My father was hurt many times from what they would say."

Although misguided at times, the surge of patriotism after Pearl Harbor enabled the country to gear up for a long struggle. Once so far away, war was now on the doorstep. Telegrams announcing the deaths of American soldiers arrived alongside Christmas cards. Even people who were not mourning relatives felt a sense of loss—and also a sense of purpose. As *Time* magazine concluded: "Japanese bombs finally brought national unity to the U.S."

America was now engaged in World War II "for the duration." On December 11, 1941, a Georgia teen named Barbara Wooddall wrote to her fiancé in the Army with a mixture of optimism and uncertainty:

> What's going to happen to us? There is no doubt in my mind as to who shall win this WAR, but how long will it take us? It makes you feel like getting the best of everything before it's all gone.

# THE HOME FRONT
# GOES TO WORK

*Don't let them catch us with our plants down!*
—Government slogan, 1940s

The day after Pearl Harbor, Herman Kramer skipped work and flew his own small plane from Maryland to Pennsylvania to enlist in the Army Air Corps. Flooded with volunteers, the army turned him down. In the first year of the war, the military didn't accept fathers, and Kramer had two children. The next day, when he returned to his job at the Westinghouse Electric plant (which was making aircraft transmitters), Kramer recalls how his boss "raised a fuss":

> "Kramer, don't you have any better sense than to go to try to enlist? Don't you think you're going to do good here? Aren't you doing something for the war effort here? Without materials, where would the Allies be?"

*Enlistees await processing at a New York City army induction center.*

Caught unprepared by the Japanese, the United States had to work quickly to provide its armed forces with basic supplies, from uniforms and helmets to tanks and ships. Fortunately, the defense industry had a head start. In 1939, lawmakers had allowed U.S. manufacturers to sell weapons to Britain and France if they paid cash. As the situation in Europe grew more desperate, payment became less important than helping friends oppose Hitler. In March 1941, Congress passed the Lend-Lease Act, authorizing the president to sell, lend, lease, or transfer equipment to U.S. allies. "We must be the great arsenal of democracy," said FDR in a "fireside chat" broadcast over the radio.

The new defense business brought a welcome end to the poverty of the Great Depression of the 1930s. In 1933, unemployment in the United States stood at 24.9 percent. By 1941, with firms making everything from planes to parachutes for overseas customers, the jobless rate had fallen below 10 percent. Throughout the war, the decline continued as the demand for equipment forced factories to hire more workers. By 1944, unemployment had dipped to 1.2 percent.

Originally a farm boy, Herman Kramer found a position on the assembly line at Westinghouse. There he noticed "the boys that were in 'time study' walking around in their suits and ties and collars," and he took classes to win a promotion to their department. Time study experts watched people work, then showed them how to speed up. Every year during the war, the government awarded an honorary E for "efficient" to factories that turned out supplies quickly. The sooner new gear reached the front lines, the better chance troops had to survive.

Although Westinghouse had been manufacturing arms for several years, many other plants had to switch suddenly from making household goods to making tools of war. To supervise this change, the government created the powerful War Production Board (WPB) in January 1942. The WPB decided which factories would receive scarce rubber, tin, and silk. The board banned or limited the production of many "nonessential" items for civilians, from cars to coat hangers. Auto plants—the pioneers of mass production—were able to turn out trucks, tanks, jeeps, and amphibious (land and sea) vehicles. Smaller manufacturers loaded shells instead of bottling soft drinks or stitched mosquito nets instead of bedspreads.

During the 1930s, labor unions and management had fought bitterly about wages and working conditions. Worrying that fights would interfere with production, the federal government formed the National War Labor Board in 1942. This 12-member group, with representatives from labor, industry, and the public, met to help workers and management compromise when they disagreed. During the war, the nation's largest unions pledged not to strike. Factory owners, pleased with big profits from selling supplies to the government, allowed more union activity.

As a result, American productivity soared beyond the combined output of all other Allied and Axis countries. Calling for 60,000 planes and 45,000 tanks in 1942, FDR announced, "Let no man say it cannot be done." And it could be done. By 1944, the Willow Run aircraft factory near Detroit could finish a B-24 bomber every 63 minutes. Henry Kaiser's West Coast shipyards delivered 14 "Liberty Ships" to the navy each month.

*A war rally at the Western Electric Company in Chicago*

"It was just amazing what we were turning out," Herman Kramer recalls. "U.S. ships were hauling it over to Europe and...getting sunk... so you had to produce that much more and more." Factories operated around the clock. Few employees minded putting in 12-hour days and six- or seven-day weeks. Workers were earning good money—and extra for overtime.

## ALL WORKING FOR VICTORY

At the beginning of the war, Selective Service, the agency that drafted men into the military, put defense plant workers at the bottom of the list for service. Lee Saunders observes that some Americans took a defense job to avoid the draft:

> There were quite a few young men who suddenly developed an interest in mechanics and shipbuilding and welding and things of that sort, that they probably would not have turned to under ordinary circumstances. But the government had no objection to that. The government needed people in the shipbuilding industry as badly as it needed soldiers, maybe more so.

*Wearing oxygen masks for safety, women clean blast furnaces at U.S. Steel in Gary, Indiana.*

Soon, however, the male labor pool couldn't supply enough hands for both combat and factory work. Women filled the gap on the home front.

Although women had made up about a quarter of the labor force in the 1930s, tradition dictated that they should keep house and raise children. The few employment opportunities open to women—nurse, secretary, maid, teacher—paid less than male positions that required equal or less skill. Also, many schools and businesses refused to hire married women. According to historian Susan Hartmann, author of *The Home Front and Beyond*, before the war "those wives who worked outside the home were viewed as selfish, greedy women who took jobs away from male breadwinners." By the end of the war, however, more than 18 million women—one-fourth of them married—held jobs.

Convincing Americans that women should put down the knitting needles and pick up the blowtorch required skillful public relations. Both sexes considered factory work "unfeminine," especially since safety regulations required women to wear pants (or a uniform) instead of dresses and to pull back their long hair with nets or bandanas. The government's Office of War Information (OWI) tried to change opinions by feeding articles to newspapers and magazines about "noble" young women giving up the comforts of home to fill the shoes of absent men.

Defense plants ran confidence-boosting ads. "If you've followed recipes exactly in making cakes, you can learn to load shell," one said. Or, "If you can drive a car, you can run a machine." Lockheed Aircraft's famous "Rosie the Riveter," a poster girl in kerchief and overalls, symbolized a new notion of American beauty. On the cover of the *Saturday Evening Post*, illustrator Norman Rockwell showed Rosie to be grimy, muscular, and full of can-do spirit.

Women performed well at their new jobs, and their presence improved working conditions for all employees. Many factories added restrooms, cafeterias, and counselors. All workers benefited from the conveyor belts, elevators, and cranes that were installed to lessen the brute strength needed on the assembly line. But the reality of "Rosie the Riveter" was more complicated than the picture presented by the media. Christine Kramer, who had been a housewife before Pearl Harbor, took a test at a Nashville, Tennessee, factory and qualified to drill, cut, and stack heavy aluminum sheeting. She says, "There was a lot of resentment with the men, because some of the women made as much money as they did."

Although the National War Labor Board pushed for equal pay for equal work, women were actually paid about 40 percent less than their male colleagues. But factory jobs still offered a step up for the women

*These Burbank, California, boys were among thousands of schoolchildren employed in aircraft production during World War II.*

who left traditionally female occupations. In Detroit, for instance, laundresses and chambermaids earned about $27 a week, while female defense workers took in $40.35. There were other rewards too—the challenge of learning a trade, the hope of speeding an Allied victory. The story of seaman Elgin Staples was well publicized. Swept overboard when his ship sunk off the Pacific island of Guadalcanal, Staples floated to safety thanks to a life preserver that had been inspected, packed, and stamped by his mother in Akron, Ohio.

Married women pulled double duty. Before or after a full day on the assembly line, they were expected to shop, cook, and clean. The government opened about 2,800 child-care centers, but most mothers had to fend for themselves. Christine Kramer, who worked from midnight to 8:00 A.M., entrusted her two kids to her sister at night. Women with less reliable baby-sitters missed shifts or quit.

The labor shortage created opportunities for other Americans who previously had few job options. Even before the raid on Pearl Harbor, black Americans had been migrating in large numbers from the rural

South to the industrial North and West. Yet racial discrimination blocked their entry into defense work and other well-paying jobs. Many blacks ended up as janitors, servants, or cooks. In the spring of 1941, A. Philip Randolph, a prominent black leader, called for a peaceful march on Washington to protest discrimination in the defense industry. Eager to avoid a confrontation, FDR established the Fair Employment Practices Committee, which would investigate complaints when workers felt they had been treated unfairly.

Civil rights organizations such as the Urban League helped argue the case of black workers. But while government and community pressure did open some doors, it could not erase prejudice. Many companies refused to hire African Americans, claiming that white employees wouldn't work alongside blacks. But the need for competent, willing hands spurred change. In Baltimore in 1942, about 9,000 black Americans worked in manufacturing. By 1944, nearly 36,000 did.

By mid-war, industry was searching for job applicants in overlooked corners. Many states suspended their child labor laws, and teens wired

*Trackwomen with the B & O Railroad, 1943*

*With her husband at war, a Michigan woman runs the family farm.*

switchboards and wove camouflage netting with adults. As a way out
of prison, convicts volunteered for military service or factory jobs.
Americans with handicaps made the most of their abilities. The deaf, for
instance, operated machinery that was too noisy for other workers.

American servicemen, or "GIs," sometimes resented the ample paychecks and "easy life" of defense workers. But factory hands were taking
risks, too. Although safety inspectors prowled the plants checking ropes
and testing gas masks, accidents happened. People suffered burns from
molten magnesium, got sick from toxic chemical fumes, and lost hair,
fingers, and limbs in machinery. Under pressure to increase production,
inexperienced staffers hurried and sometimes were hurt by dangerous
equipment. By January 1944, the number of personal injuries on the
job had topped those on the battlefield.

Although the defense industry received the most publicity, other em-
ployers called upon the talents of a diverse work force. Women operated
the pumps at gas stations, delivered mail for the post office, edited local
newspapers, and drove garbage trucks, taxis, and ambulances. African
Americans met more resistance but succeeded in entering new fields. In
1944, when the city of Philadelphia hired eight black trolley-car operators, white drivers called an illegal strike. Since defense workers depended
on public transportation, President Roosevelt ordered 8,000 troops into
the city to keep the buses and trolley cars running—with blacks and
whites at the wheel.

## FARM WORK IS WAR WORK

Since the Lend-Lease Act, American agriculture had been feeding the
Allies. As a government slogan put it, "Food will win the war and write
the peace." Selective Service granted deferments—permission to skip
military service—to farm owners. Most field hands, however, were drafted
or moved to cities for better-paying jobs. Once again, women and young
people pitched in to fill a gap.

Housewives in rural areas canned fruits and vegetables for the military, and college students spent summers in the barnyard. At harvest
time in the fall, county schools let out so kids and teachers could gather

*High school boys gather barley on a Maryland farm.*

the crops. In 1943, the government set up the U.S. Crop Corps. Part of its mission was to convince farm managers that female farm workers could handle tractors and combines, as well as heat, dust, and low wages. Thanks in part to this "Women's Land Army," American agriculture prospered in the early 1940s.

## ALTERNATE SERVICE

Conscientious objectors—men who refused to fight on religious or moral grounds—performed unpaid "alternate service" on the home front. About 12,000 conscientious objectors (COs) lived in 151 Civilian Public Service camps, established by the government and run by three pacifist churches—the Quakers, the Brethren, and the Mennonites. Public service work ranged from planting trees to training as "smoke jumpers," fire fighters who parachuted into burning forests. Many conscientious objectors cared for patients in mental hospitals. At least 500 COs volunteered for military medical experiments, agreeing to be starved, infected with malaria, or infested by lice. Yet many Americans called COs cowards. One barber near a public service camp in New Hampshire posted a sign: No Yellow Bellies, Conscientious Objectors or Skunks Allowed in Here.

But everybody in the United States knew that their hardships paled beside those of soldiers and sailors under enemy fire. Westinghouse posted the names of all employees who had been drafted—where they were and whether they had died. Herman Kramer didn't envy the troops in the mountains of Europe or the jungles of Asia. "The war to us—the ones that stayed home—was an exciting time of life," he explains.

"It was like dark and daylight from the Depression to the war," Christine Kramer agrees. "Because you were making money."

*Lunchtime at a CO camp*

# AMERICA TIGHTENS ITS BELT

*Use it up, wear it out, make it do, or do without.*

　　—Home-front saying, 1940s

In the 1940s, prosperity and scarcity went hand in hand. During the Depression, many Americans were poor, but those who had money could buy whatever they wanted. During the war, however, the government had first claim on food and raw materials, from applesauce to zinc. The needs of the soldiers outweighed any inconvenience to the home front. Even rich civilians could no longer buy every comfort.

On overdrive after Pearl Harbor, war production guzzled metals, rubber, and gasoline. By early 1942, Japan had cut off the world's main supply of rubber by overrunning Malaya, a British colony in the South China Sea. The United States was left scrambling to import latex (sap from rubber trees) from Brazil or to make synthetic rubber. In June 1942, President Roosevelt begged the public to scrounge for old tires, garden hose, and rubber gloves. Within a month, civilians had collected 450,000 tons of used rubber, much of which was melted down and remolded.

The successful scrap drive for rubber led to drives for metal and paper, prompting singer Bing Crosby to croon, "Junk Will Win the War." But recycling alone could not eliminate shortages. German U-boats were sinking oil tankers. Ships that once carried coffee from South to North America instead were crossing the Atlantic with war matériel. Outfitting millions of draftees with combat boots depleted leather supplies.

The government worried that shortages would make prices on the home front rise higher and higher—with scarce goods going to the highest bidder, like at an auction. To prevent rising prices, the federal Office of Price Administration (OPA) took two major steps in 1942. First, the OPA set price limits on everything from soup to rent. Second, the agency began to ration (restrict purchases of) essential goods such as sugar, coffee, and gas. Soon rationing extended to shoes, meat, fish, flour, and canned goods. Each person was entitled to two pounds of sugar a month, for instance, and three pairs of shoes a year.

Families picked up ration coupon books at neighborhood schools. Each red or blue coupon was worth a certain number of "points." The OPA allowed every American 64 red points (for meat, butter, and fats) and 48 blue points (for processed foods like ketchup) every month. At the store, grocers tagged food by price and point. A pound of pork chops might cost 38 cents and eight red points, depending on the cut and how much pork was available.

Gas rations varied with need. Most people qualified for an "A" sticker—four (later three) gallons a week, enough for trips to the market but not for a Sunday drive in the country. Commuters, such as defense workers in a car pool, received a bigger allowance with "B" stickers. Farmers with heavy machinery to run were allowed even more. Doctors, police officers, and other emergency workers could stop at the gas pump anytime. To the outrage of struggling motorists, members of Congress voted themselves "X" stickers for unlimited fill-ups.

*Lining up for rationed sugar*

GASOLINE RATION

*Most Americans displayed this sticker in their car windows.*

Local ration boards, staffed mainly by volunteers, assigned the gas alphabet as well as heating oil allowances, which were calculated according to the size of a house and the number of children in it. People had to make special requests to purchase cars, trucks, stoves, tires, typewriters, and other items. Fishermen, for instance, had to apply for a new pair of rubber hip boots.

Ration boards also investigated reports of cheating, often filed by overly patriotic or busybody neighbors. In some communities, board members acted like parents, telling people what they could and could not do. As one woman complained to writer Archie Satterfield, "They were always saying dumb things like, 'Don't you know there's a war on?'"

That phrase popped up often, part sigh, part laugh. No shopper could ever forget there was a war on. With steel blades at a premium, lawn mowers disappeared for the duration of the war, as did ice skates. (In 1943, skater Sonja Henie took out a $250,000 insurance policy on her five remaining pairs.) On birthdays, kids received no bicycles or rubber balls. Even toy trains were made out of cardboard. Imports of everything from spices to glass eyes halted because ships had more important cargo to transport to the troops. Stores frequently ran out of bobby pins, can openers, and batteries, whose copper, zinc, and lead were needed for arms production. Providing for troops first meant those on the home front had to wait in line for leftovers—lines for cigarettes, lines for fabric, lines for whiskey, lines for stockings.

Shortages and rationing had far-reaching effects. To conserve cloth and metal, dressmakers shortened hems and eliminated cuffs, hoods, and zippers. Pennies turned gray as the U.S. Mint replaced the copper coating with zinc, and, by the end of the war, some coins were made of spent shell casings. Motels and drive-in restaurants suffered because Americans couldn't buy much gas for their cars. To save gas and rubber tires, dairies reduced home milk delivery to every other day.

Because Selective Service had drafted so many loggers, fewer trees reached paper mills. On the theory that reading improved morale, the

*Tires to be melted and remolded for use in war vehicles*

*Even with ration stickers and coupons, Americans could not always buy what they needed.*

War Production Board steered adequate paper stock to newspapers and magazines. But big hardcover books gave way to pocket paperbacks. Recalling his boyhood in Archie Satterfield's *The Home Front*, Don Lanskov remembered a neighbor, "an otherwise normal, modest woman," running down the street and yelling: "'There's toilet paper at the A&P!'"

## DOING WITHOUT—OR BUYING ON THE SLY

Some Americans resented the hardships imposed by war. Esther Benson, then a mother of three young boys, told writer Roy Hoopes:

> Rationing was awful, awful. I was always losing the ration books, and you just couldn't get anything good, even if you did have the ration coupons. I remember thinking a can of corned beef was just marvelous. We ate a lot of Spam.

Complaining didn't change the situation, though, so most people made the best of things. Esther Benson's husband caught fish from his sailboat to put more food on the table. "Gas was rationed, so you just planned," Sylvia Choate explains. "You walked. You bicycled. You doubled up. You took turns."

Menus couldn't always be planned, however, no matter how carefully homemakers spent their points. If the butcher had no hamburger, a cook had to improvise with unrationed liver, mutton, or horse meat. *Gourmet* magazine sympathized with its readers:

> Although it isn't
> Our usual habit,
> This year we're eating
> The Easter Rabbit.

Women's magazines also tailored their recipes for rations, substituting margarine for butter or corn syrup for sugar. Although some of these concoctions flopped, others surprised the skeptical. "I remember making bread with mineral oil because you couldn't get any kind of shortening," Christine Kramer says. "Everybody thought, boy, we'll be going to the bathroom. But it didn't affect us."

Supplementing rations became a national pastime. Encouraged by the government, homeowners planted more than 20 million backyard "Victory Gardens," which yielded a third of the total U.S. vegetable crop in 1943. Many families canned fruits and vegetables, and some people hunted. By 1943 anyone could earn bonus points by saving bacon grease and other kitchen fats and dumping them in official scrap barrels. (The glycerin in fats was an ingredient used to make explosives.)

The hard times of the 1930s had trained many Americans to scrimp, scrounge, and improvise. During the war, smokers once again rolled their own cigarettes, and farmers patched their grain sacks. Secretaries, unable to buy silk or nylon hose, put makeup on their legs to resemble seamed stockings. Businesses experimented too. At least one newspaper hired a horse and carriage to deliver the morning edition. Manufacturers replaced brass with glass and steel with plastics. But when the metal shortage forced a Pennsylvania hospital to resort to taping the diapers of newborns, the local Lions Club rounded up 6,000 used safety pins.

Many people bent OPA rules. Some farmers butchered part of their herd in the woods and peddled beef on the sly. Friends swapped coupons, and grocers sometimes set aside steak or other wartime delicacies for their best customers. Cigarettes earned the nickname "stoopies," because merchants had to stoop down to pull out the packs they had stashed under the counter.

The illegal "black market" included sales of coal, butter, wristwatches, garbage cans—anything scarce. Alice Marriott told writer Roy Hoopes that at her corner store in Washington, D.C., she could get anything she wanted, but "we paid through the nose." Usually, though, dealing with "Mr. Black" required more sneaking around. A person in search of extra gas would ask quietly, and word of mouth would lead to someone selling ration stamps that had been bought, stolen, or forged. Although many black marketeers operated on a small scale, gangsters also joined in this profitable trade. They stole and resold everything from spare parts to tires stripped from cars. Many Americans shunned the black market as both criminal and unpatriotic.

The one thing that might have tempted law-abiding citizens wasn't available on the black market: housing. War rearranged the population. According to the Census Bureau, 15.3 million Americans moved in the early 1940s, half of them to different states. Wives and girlfriends followed servicemen to camps and bases all over the country. Workers migrated from farms and small towns to big cities and out-of-the-way places where huge new factories created instant communities. Although the War Production Board permitted the construction of modest houses near defense plants, the building industry couldn't keep pace with the new arrivals.

At the government's urging, many families emptied a room and took in renters. Even so, finding a bed was far more difficult than finding a job. Newcomers slept in crowded apartments, dormitories, boardinghouses —even shacks. In Mobile, Alabama, some workers paid a quarter to rent a cot for eight hours.

*Hollywood stars encouraged Americans to conserve and recycle. Rita Hayworth donated her car bumpers to the war effort.*

*Home-front scrap collections*

In a well-known joke of the time, a passerby hears a drowning man (named Joe) cry for help. Instead of rescuing Joe, the passerby finds out his address and runs to Joe's landlord, asking to rent a room. "Sorry," the landlord says when the panting fellow knocks on the door. "The guy who pushed Joe in just took it."

## THE COST OF VICTORY

Mobilizing the nation for war was expensive. Paying troops and buying equipment like arms and uniforms cost about $330 billion over four years. The U.S. Treasury borrowed some of this money from banks, but at least a third came from citizens. Most people loaned money to the government by buying war bonds, certificates that promised to repay the purchase price, plus interest. To buy a $25 bond, for instance, a person paid the government $18.75. Ten years later, the bondholder received $25.

The fund-raisers promoted war bonds less as an investment than as a patriotic duty. Magazines ran public service ads: "Back the Attack with War Bonds." Celebrities—even Superman—traveled the country urging Americans to support the war. Actress Hedy Lamarr, dubbed the most beautiful woman in the world, promised to kiss anyone who purchased $25,000 worth of bonds. Americans were generous. When Kate Smith, the beloved singer of "God Bless America," went on the radio in September 1943 to urge listeners to buy war bonds, the government collected almost $40 million in one day.

The Treasury didn't scorn small contributions, though. Knocking on doors, children collected dimes and quarters to buy war stamps, which were pasted into albums. An album full of stamps could be traded for a $25 bond. "We were using our allowances ... and whatever way we could to get money," Ray Hartman recalled in *Americans Remember the Home Front*. In nine months, students at his Chicago school raised about $80,000, the price of a P-38 fighter plane. "Alphonsus was the name of the school," he said, "but they named the plane The Spirit of Saint Al's."

To cover the rest of its expenses, the government levied an extra five-percent "Victory Tax" on personal income and took a big bite out of corporate profits. "Pay Your Taxes, Beat the Axis," a slogan said. Workers didn't have much choice. The government eliminated the once-per-year income tax payment and began withholding taxes from monthly and weekly paychecks. Since employment was up, more Americans paid taxes.

**BUY WAR BONDS**

*With food in short supply, Americans filled out their menus with produce from their own gardens.*

Between 1940 and 1945, the taxpayer rolls grew from 7 million to 42 million people.

Although all the new regulations complicated life on the home front, they also kept the nation busy and focused on its goal: victory. While the poverty of the 1930s had defeated spirits, the challenges of the 1940s seemed to raise them.

Along with wartime hit songs like "When the Lights Go on Again," Americans hummed Beethoven's Fifth Symphony since the opening notes (da, da, da, duuum) sounded like the Morse code "V" ( . . . -)—for victory. Local defense councils awarded certificates to "V-Homes," households that obeyed the air raid warden, lowered the thermostat, salvaged aluminum pans, and bought war bonds. Americans planted Victory Gardens, paid Victory Taxes, and, at a five-and-dime in New York City, even bought "Victory Socks." In 1943, many workers were reporting late to their shifts, in part because the War Production Board had phased out alarm clocks. The WPB realized it had made a mistake and phased the clocks back in. Soon 1.75 million timepieces were rolling off the assembly lines— the "Victory Model," of course.

# LONG TIME NO SEE

*Of all the sad words of tongue*
*   or pen,*
*The saddest are these:*
*   There are no men.*
> —Popular saying, 1940s

In 1942, the war was going badly for the Allies. In the Pacific, battered American forces surrendered the last of the Philippine islands to the Japanese. In Europe, the Germans had advanced as far as Stalingrad in the Soviet Union. "We weren't sure what would happen," BettyLou Folley says. "It was touch and go there." Although most civilians believed the United States would triumph in the end, no one knew the price of victory—how much time, how much blood.

Between 1940 and 1945, roughly 16 million Americans served in the armed forces. Almost every family sent someone near and dear into the fray. BettyLou Folley's mother, like so many others across the country,

*A family in Lehighton, Pennsylvania, displays eight stars honoring eight sons in uniform.*

posted two blue stars—one for each son in the military—on a white banner in her window. "We didn't have yellow ribbons," Folley explains. "We just had the stars."

Saying goodbye was a continual drama on the home front. As draftees left for boot camp, towns organized send-off bashes at the train station, with parades of high school bands. Many soldiers and sailors returned home on leave between assignments, at least until the high command shipped them overseas. It was a time of comings and goings, of happy reunions and painful farewells.

Even the servicemen who remained in the United States—and at least one-quarter of them did for the entirety of the war—were usually stationed far from home. Without friends or relatives nearby, thousands of lonely young men wandered into town on Saturday nights—and many ended up drinking, fighting, and carousing with prostitutes. To draw business away from the saloons and tattoo parlors, civic leaders invited military men and women to dances, church canteens (socials), and variety shows sponsored by the United Service Organizations (USO).

The USO was a joint venture of the government and private groups such as the Young Men's Christian Association and the National Jewish Welfare Board. The USO operated about 3,000 clubs in or near military installations in the U.S., as well as 10 overseas. Big-name celebrities—comedian Bob Hope, dancers Fred Astaire and Ginger Rogers, movie stars like Humphrey Bogart and Joan Crawford—traveled to the front lines to perform in USO shows. At the Stage Door Canteen in New York City, Broadway and Hollywood stars dropped in between nine and midnight to serenade a throng in uniform. Outside of big cities, entertainment tended to be more homespun: At Fort Riley, Kansas, the USO arranged for soldiers to spend weekends with local farm families.

The government endorsed the USO because it kept troops cheerful and out of trouble. But civilian volunteers, both for the USO and other civic groups, donated their time and talents for a simpler reason: Every GI Joe or Jane could be their own son or daughter, brother or sister.

Young women were invited—sometimes by the busload—to dances with soldiers in high school gyms and hotel ballrooms around the country. BettyLou Folley signed up as a "hostess" with the New York City Defense Recreation Committee. Once every six weeks, Folley reported to the Hotel Commodore. Wearing ribbons pinned to their dresses, the hostesses mingled with officers and made small talk.

"It was exciting to meet these servicemen in their uniforms," Folley recalls. "We'd all sit at tables. You'd meet the fellas that way, and they'd ask you to dance. And if you hit it off, you'd have a couple of dates I suppose."

Most parents didn't mind their daughters keeping company with servicemen at chaperoned activities. Many Americans in uniform wanted friendship as much as romance—someone to talk to and correspond with.

Letter writing, once a common practice in the United States, had fallen out of fashion after 1920. The telephone and automobile offered easier ways to keep in touch. During World War II, with loved ones an ocean away and long-distance calls in the United States limited to five minutes by 1943, letters made a comeback. Magazines gave readers tips

*Letter writing improved morale at home and overseas.*

*Servicemen meet women at a USO dance.*

on how to write happy, newsy notes to soldiers, and many teens competed to see who could get the most pen pals.

The government encouraged letter writing because it boosted morale. After March 1942, soldiers no longer had to pay for postage, except airmail, which cost six cents per half ounce. The Post Office was humming. In 1940, it handled about 28 million pieces of mail; in 1945, about 38 billion. Since letters took up precious cargo space on ships, the government introduced three-cent "V-Mail." By microfilming short letters written on special stationery, the Army Signal Corps could reduce 2,575 pounds of paper to 45 pounds of film reels. Original letters were kept on file in case of a mishap with the film. Officials on the receiving end, abroad or at home, enlarged and printed the negatives for delivery.

## "I LEFT MY HEART AT THE STAGE DOOR CANTEEN"

Many young people fell in love during World War II. Uncertainty about the future added a sense of urgency to everyday events. In an interview for *The Homefront*, Patricia Livermore described the early 1940s as "a very hectic, exciting time, but there was always an underlying sadness.... Relationships were extremely intense, because you didn't know how long they would last."

Americans married at a record rate. In the five months after Pearl Harbor, 1,000 couples tied the knot each day. Some men hoped to avoid military service, since married men were exempt from the draft until 1943. Some women looked forward to the $50 monthly government allotment for servicemen's wives. In fact, by leading more than one soldier to the altar, a few "Allotment Annies" collected as much as $300 per month—not to mention a $10,000 life insurance payment if one of their GI husbands died.

Many couples felt pressure to marry, or at least to have sex. As one popular song put it, "You Can't Say No to a Soldier."

"The idea was, well, let's live for today because I may not come back tomorrow," Lee Saunders explains. "I'll marry this girl now: I'm not all that crazy about her, but I don't want to go over alone."

Yet many Americans made genuine promises to each other as a way of affirming love and life in a period darkened by death. Typical was the whirlwind courtship of a secretary and a soldier in the movie *The Clock* (1945). At crowded Grand Central Station, Alice Mayberry (played by Judy Garland) trips over the leg of Joe Allen (Robert Walker), an army corporal with a two-day leave. She agrees, somewhat reluctantly, to show him around New York City. After they almost lose each other on the subway, they decide to marry.

Racing against the clock, they fill out forms and take a blood test— and catch the justice of the peace just as he's leaving for the day. With no rings and no witnesses but the janitors, Alice and Joe exchange vows. Afterwards, over dinner in a cafeteria, the letdown catches up with them. They hardly know each other. Joe flips to a photo of his mother in his wallet. "So you think she'll like me?" Alice asks.

Although the movie ends with a sense that Mr. and Mrs. Allen will honor their commitment to each other, their frantic goodbye at the station leaves the audience guessing: No one knows if Joe will survive the war unharmed.

*Before shipping out to Europe, airmen peer out from a bomber at Connecticut's Bradley Field.*

The rash of "hurry-up" weddings worried older Americans, especially those military commanders who preferred that fighting men stay single and undistracted. But youth prevailed. "All my friends who were engaged or about to be engaged speeded up their weddings much faster than it had been prewar, where you became engaged, you were engaged for a year, then got married," says Sylvia Choate.

War shortened ceremonies, too. Many brides and grooms lined up at city halls or chapels. Even traditional weddings had an improvised quality. Servicemen juggled plans long-distance with their fiancées, who kept caterers, ministers, and bridesmaids on hold. Sandy Whitman, then a naval lieutenant in Chicago, remembers requesting leave from his commanding officer to marry Sylvia Choate in Boston in 1943: "[The officer] said, 'It says here you had leave last summer.' And I said, 'I did. That

*A farewell kiss as the army's 165th Regiment departs from Hoboken, New Jersey*

was to get engaged. This is to get married.'" The commander eventually agreed to grant Whitman leave, but warned, "You have no more than 24 hours in Boston." Sandy and Sylvia were married within 20. Their honeymoon was the train ride back to Chicago.

Despite official advice to stay home, many military wives followed their husbands in hopes of spending Sundays and the occasional weekend together. War brides rented cramped rooms in towns near bases. To keep busy, they gave blood, packed boxes for the Red Cross, and volunteered in hospitals, which needed help because so many of the medical staff had been sent overseas.

Heeding the advice of Barbara Klaw, author of the 1943 best-seller *Camp Follower: The Story of a Soldier's Wife*, many brides lived out of a trunk. They were usually on the move. If transferred, a serviceman was guaranteed a seat on a crowded train or bus, but his wife had to fend for herself. Although rarely a treat, the travel was an adventure for many women, most of whom had never gone far from home.

In the midst of this upheaval, babies arrived—one million from 1941 to 1945. As husbands shipped out overseas, sometimes before the birth of their children, wives became single parents. They washed diapers in the sink, warmed bottles late at night, and tried, through their letters, to link father and child. As Ethel Gorman counseled in her 1943 book, *So Your Husband's Gone to War*, wives wrote more about their joys than their burdens.

## THE ULTIMATE SACRIFICE

The United States suffered fewer casualties than other Allied countries during World War II, but the losses—more than 400,000 troops killed and 670,000 wounded—devastated the home front. "A dozen died in our neighborhood," remembers Christine Kramer. "And you wondered who was going to be next."

Both Kramer's brothers were drafted, and boys she had known in high school were dying: one at Pearl Harbor, one in a mine field, one in an accident, one at sea. "When one of your buddies got killed, you heard about that," she says. "You grieved about that for a month. And about the time you got over that, there'd be another one. . . . That really tore us up."

Bad news arrived in telegrams from the War Department: "REGRET TO INFORM YOU YOUR SON . . . SERIOUSLY WOUNDED IN ACTION." In case of a death, the Red Cross might ask a minister or neighbor to stand by during the delivery of the yellow envelope.

Commanding officers usually sent a prompt letter of sympathy to the family of a man or woman killed in action. But the body itself was often buried temporarily—or for good—in foreign soil. Loved ones could wait weeks, sometimes months, for the details of a tragedy. The War Department sent updates about hospitalized GIs, but there was little information about the missing. "War ages you fast," Dorothy Schenck told writer Roy Hoopes. "No night did you sleep." When news of her son's capture finally reached home, she sent him a care package via the Red Cross. It wasn't until months after the end of the war that Schenck learned her son had died on a ship accidentally bombed by Americans.

War brought sadness into every American's life. Local newspapers ran lists of casualties. Radio stations and magazines reported stories of people like the Sullivans of Waterloo, Iowa. After hearing of a friend's death at Pearl Harbor, the five Sullivan sons enlisted in the navy—and died together when a torpedo blasted their cruiser, the U.S.S. *Juneau*, off Guadalcanal.

Letters teens sent to their pen pals returned stamped "Deceased." When one serviceman didn't write as promised, BettyLou Folley contacted the War Department. "He was so beautiful and handsome, a pilot," she recalls. "They wrote back that he was shot down and killed the month after he went over there. So that was a shock to me, even though I hadn't known him very long."

War claimed celebrities, too: the Lone Ranger, radio star Lee Beriian Powell; orchestra leader Glenn Miller; and journalist Ernie Pyle, age 42. Pyle's newspaper columns and best-selling books (*Here Is Your War*, 1943; *Brave Men*, 1944) about regular GI Joes won him—and the troops— a nation of fans. At the factory where Christine Kramer was employed, the management relayed breaking news over the loudspeaker. "When

Ernie Pyle got killed" in 1945, she remembers, "everybody stopped working."

As families looked for meaning in their sacrifice, the sale of religious books, particularly the Bible, soared. Attendance at worship services also grew during World War II. The sense that the community mourned together helped to ease grief and bitterness. When a soldier was killed, his widow or mother replaced the blue star in her window with a gold one, a badge of honor as well as sorrow.

Mostly, World War II was a period of suspense, of praying for the best and accepting the worst. As BettyLou Folley says, the war "changed my life because all the fellas were away. It wasn't a normal life. You were just waiting, waiting, waiting. Waiting for the day the war would be over."

*Journalist Ernie Pyle was killed on the Pacific island of Okinawa in 1945.*

# A COUNTRY UNITED AND DIVIDED

*Se sirve solamente a raza blanca.*
*(Only the white race served.)*
— Sign in Los Angeles
restaurants, 1940s

The home front looked to Washington for leadership. Despite his upper-class roots, Franklin Delano Roosevelt had impressed Americans of all backgrounds with his courage in fighting polio and his compassion for the "forgotten man." He had guided the United States through the Great Depression. In 1940 voters reelected FDR to a third term in office.

At his first inauguration in 1933, a time of hunger and panic, he had assured the public that "the only thing we have to fear is fear itself." Eight years later, with the U.S. economy recovering but the world situation deteriorating, he once again inspired Americans with his take-charge attitude. In his 1941 State of the Union address, he told Congress:

> In the future days, which we seek to make secure, we look
> forward to a world grounded on four essential freedoms. . . .
> Freedom of speech and expression . . . freedom of every person
> to worship God in his own way . . . freedom from want . . . freedom
> from fear.

Ironically, in an effort to defend freedom, the federal government suspended many civil liberties for the duration of the war. The confinement
of families of Japanese ancestry was the most extreme example. Yet
Washington exerted control over the lives of almost all Americans.

After Pearl Harbor, the government screened all letters that might
affect national defense. "Yes, your private mail could be read," says Lee
Saunders. He worked briefly for the U.S. Bureau of Censorship, sorting
letters into piles based on country of origin—Germany, Italy, Japan,
China. His superiors opened anything suspicious, hoping to intercept
spy messages or to trace leaks of sensitive information.

"I think the main thing that they were concerned about in those days
had to do with shipping," Saunders says. "The routes of ships, when
they were leaving, where they were headed, what they were carrying,
and how they were protected."

Opposite: *Mexican Ameri-
can youths arrested for
rioting in Los Angeles.*
Right: *The Office of War
Information warned that
leaked secrets could cost
American lives.*

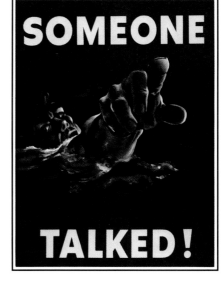

The military also closely guarded its battle plans. At overseas bases, officers read soldiers' outgoing mail and cut out with scissors any dates or place names that might reveal a battle plan. Folks back home soon grew accustomed to "swiss-cheese" letters. The media also cooperated with military censors, delaying stories and obscuring details to protect troops in the field. "We just took it in stride; it was part of the war," BettyLou Folley says.

Not even veteran news-hounds caught the scent of the greatest story on the home front: the "Manhattan Project"—the race to build the world's first atomic bomb. In utmost secrecy, General Leslie Groves coordinated the project, picking Berkeley professor J. Robert Oppenheimer as the lead physicist. Building the bomb was a complicated puzzle. For secrecy's sake, the task was divided into pieces, and most workers had no idea how their part fit into the whole. Like all defense workers though, they were told to keep their mouths shut—"Loose Lips Sink Ships." All Manhattan Project participants risked a $10,000 fine and ten years in prison just for talking about what they were doing.

Finally, Oppenheimer and a team of scientists put all the pieces together at an isolated camp in Los Alamos, New Mexico. By figuring out how to set off a nuclear chain reaction, they were able to release the tremendous energy of the atom. After the first test of the bomb on July 16, 1945, people within 300 miles of the blast in the New Mexico desert reported seeing the flash. But the president didn't want to announce this super-weapon just yet. To stifle curiosity, army officials announced that an ammunition dump had exploded.

## "ACC-CENT-CHU-ATE THE POSITIVE"

While the government kept secrets, it nonetheless tried to inform the public about home-front programs—and spread optimistic messages. As the public relations agency for the federal government, the Office of War Information fed facts and suggestions to the media. For instance, OWI's Domestic News Bureau published *Victory Bulletin*, full of upbeat stories and illustrations that newspapers, radio stations, and magazines could use for free.

*The home front was hungry for articles about the war. But the government often "whitewashed," or glossed over, grim battle news to maintain morale.*

When the conversion to war production eliminated many consumer goods, the advertising industry suffered. Unemployed artists and copy-writers were eager to work for OWI. The agency produced posters with slogans such as "Avenge December 7" or "For Freedom's Sake, Buy War Bonds." In one image, a Rosie the Riveter in kerchief and uniform rolls up her sleeve and insists, "We Can Do It!" In another poster, a soldier clasps the shoulder of a farm boy and says, "Those overalls are your uniform, Bud." Throughout the war, the OWI cast the enemy as evildoers: cold-blooded "Huns" who plunged daggers into Bibles, leering "Japs" who chased innocent women. As Herman Kramer remembers, "The propaganda kept everybody geared up."

Many moviemakers wrote their scripts according to government guidelines. Americans adored the "flicks," buying 55 to 80 million tickets every week during 1942. Theaters near large defense plants held showings 24 hours a day for workers coming off and on shifts. While romances and mysteries allowed viewers to escape from the world's troubles for a few hours, the home front also hungered for war stories. In Hollywood, OWI's Bureau of Motion Pictures urged directors and screenwriters to portray the valor of the Allies. Combat films such as *Air Force* (1943), *The Purple Heart* (1944), and *The Story of G.I. Joe* (1945) kept the noble qualities of servicemen before the public.

Although exaggerated, movies and other propaganda mirrored real experiences. No film captured the quiet heroism of the home front better than *Since You Went Away* (1944). In this epic story of "the unconquerable fortress: the American Home...1943," Claudette Colbert plays a middle-class mother of two whose husband is called to active duty. Because of his salary cut (army captains earn less than advertising executives), Mrs. Hilton must budget her money, dismiss her maid, and clean her own house. Although her elder daughter, Jane, complains, "that's Communism," Mrs. Hilton rents her own bedroom to a retired colonel.

Tragedies strike in *Since You Went Away*, but characters surmount them, with the help of good people in the community. Although she faints after opening the telegram that reports her husband missing in action, Mrs. Hilton refuses to wallow in despair. Her example heartens Jane, whose fiancé (the colonel's grandson) dies in battle. Stronger, wiser Jane lays aside her grief and continues work as a nurse's aide in a ward full of amputees and veterans psychologically scarred by combat.

In *Since You Went Away*, each setback prompts a greater willingness to contribute to the war effort. Saying she hasn't made any sacrifices,

*Mrs. Hilton comforts daughter Bridget in* Since You Went Away.

Mrs. Hilton takes a welding job in a shipyard. All this virtue, of course, does not go unrewarded. At the end of the movie, just before Christmas, the family receives a cable: Captain Hilton is alive and well and coming home on leave.

Government prodding alone could not produce such grace under pressure. That spirit grew out of a sense of national unity. Patriotism was running so high during World War II that sports fans began the tradition of singing "The Star-Spangled Banner" at the start of every ball game.

War also had an equalizing effect. Rich and poor alike served in the military. Bankers and bus drivers received the same rations. Household servants quit to take factory jobs, forcing many wealthy Americans to live less grandly. Meanwhile, defense work so fattened the wallets of farmers and laborers that many could afford homes with electricity and plumbing for the first time in their lives. Strangers mingled at work, in lines, on trains, in canteens. Small kindnesses—sharing the latest news of the war or a last cigarette, for instance—made Americans from all walks of life feel a kinship.

## BURDEN OF RACISM

Tremors of discontent, however, warned that the United States was not all one big, happy family. Discrimination and poverty still divided the nation. Ever since Pearl Harbor, tension had been mounting in Los Angeles between whites and Mexican Americans. Mexican American gangs took to the streets at night in their zoot suits—flashy outfits of baggy trousers and long coats, usually worn with wide-brimmed hats— which became a costume of defiance.

The youths were called "pachucos," after Pachuca, Mexico, famous for its colorful garb. Writing from bias as much as fact, two newspapers accused the pachucos of a major crime wave. The mayor of Los Angeles called for a crackdown, and heavy-handed police officers made mass arrests of Mexican American youths, innocent teens along with street toughs.

In June 1943, a rumor that a group of young Mexican Americans had beaten up a sailor drew a mob of servicemen into downtown Los Angeles. For several nights, soldiers and sailors raided cafes and cinemas, beating anyone in zoot suits. They prowled through the *barrios*—the Mexican neighborhoods—yelling, "Kill the pachuco bastards!" Similar "zoot-suit riots" also broke out in other cities along the coast.

Even more widespread was violence between blacks and whites. In the South, where Jim Crow laws separated whites from "coloreds," townspeople often harrassed black soldiers stationed at nearby camps. Rumors, job competition, and overcrowding also sparked confrontations in factory towns. In 1942, whites in Detroit stoned and beat black workers as they moved into the Sojourner Truth housing project, located in a white neighborhood.

At a Detroit River beach in June 1943, a riot erupted from rumors that a white man had tossed a black woman and child from a bridge. Stabbings, lootings, and panic disrupted the city. At the request of the governor of Michigan, Roosevelt sent in federal troops. But by the time order was restored, 700 people had been wounded and 34 killed, most of them black.

Black leaders called their struggle a "Double V" campaign: While black soldiers were fighting the Axis abroad, black civilians were fighting prejudice at home. In the mid-1940s, the victories were symbolic. In

*Whites attack an African American man in Detroit.*

1939 the Daughters of the American Revolution had barred black singer Marian Anderson from Constitution Hall in Washington, D.C. In 1943 she performed there in a war relief fund-raising concert before an integrated audience. That year, the American Bar Association dropped a policy of excluding black lawyers. In 1944, the Supreme Court ruled that black voters had a right to vote in primary elections.

Most significantly, black Americans were organizing. They joined politically active groups such as the Urban League and the American Council on Race Relations. Between 1940 and 1945, the National Association for the Advancement of Colored People (NAACP) swelled from 50,000 to 500,000 members.

Other victims of injustice also spoke out. In a case that traveled all the way to the Supreme Court, a lawyer argued on behalf of Mitsuye Endo that the U.S. government had no right to detain loyal American citizens of Japanese ancestry. The nine Supreme Court justices agreed, and soon after their decision, in January 1945, the War Relocation Authority allowed Japanese Americans to leave relocation camps.

The American ideals about liberty and justice for all sharply contrasted with the undemocratic treatment of minorities. Writers of all races probed America's prejudices. As sociologist Gunnar Myrdal concluded in *An American Dilemma* (1944), the United States was torn because it didn't practice what it preached.

### "SPRING WILL BE A LITTLE LATE THIS YEAR"

The changes afoot during the war years alarmed conservative Americans. Not only were black people calling for a full share of freedom, but traditional families were falling apart. Some lonely brides took lovers, sending "Dear John" (I don't want to see you again) letters to their husbands overseas. Children grew up without fathers—and often with working mothers. Factory work coupled with the lack of day-care created "eight-hour orphans," kids who fended for themselves while their parents were working.

Worried social scientists pointed to juvenile delinquency as a sign of the breakdown in order. "Victory Girls," teens in bobby socks and tight

Seated left to right: *British Prime Minister Winston Churchill, Franklin D. Roosevelt, and Soviet leader Joseph Stalin meet in Yalta.*

sweaters, loitered by bars hoping to meet servicemen. Boys roamed city streets in gangs. In Seattle, Washington, acts of gang violence pushed city leaders to enforce a 9:00 P.M. winter curfew for kids under 16. People wondered what was happening to traditional morals and whether the United States would ever return to "normal" after the war.

Americans were further shaken by the death of President Roosevelt on April 12, 1945. Sitting for a portrait at his retreat in Warm Springs, Georgia, he suffered a brain hemorrhage. "I have a terrific headache," he said, and then he collapsed.

For two years, the president's health had been failing, but he hadn't cut back his schedule. In fact, he had sought and won a fourth term in office. His hands had shaken as he read his short inaugural speech. In February 1945, with the Nazis in retreat across Europe, the Allied leaders had met to discuss the terms for the German surrender. Photos of this meeting, held in Yalta on the Crimean Peninsula, showed a thin, weary 63-year-old Roosevelt. But reporters hadn't commented much in print about his decline. BettyLou Folley remembers:

> I was coming home on the bus from work, and I heard people talking that the president had died. And I was so shocked. . . . He hadn't been well. Pictures in the paper and the newsreel showed him meeting with . . . Stalin and Churchill. . . . When his death came, it was still a great shock to us. And we all mourned for a long, long time.

As a train carried the president's body back to the capital, people lined the tracks. Some sang spirituals and others heaped flowers on the coffin at every station. As the president's body lay in state at the White House, thousands of Americans attended memorial services in cities across the country. After a ceremony in Washington, another train carried the casket to Hyde Park, New York, where Franklin Delano Roosevelt was buried at his family estate.

British Prime Minister Winston Churchill once remarked that meeting FDR was "like opening a bottle of champagne." Saying goodbye left America flat. "Everybody adored the president," Herman Kramer says. "He was our father."

# THE AMERICAN CENTURY DAWNS

*The peoples of the earth face the
future with grave uncertainty....
They look to the United States as
never before for good will, strength,
and wise leadership.*
—President Harry Truman, 1949

Franklin Delano Roosevelt missed by less than a month the German
surrender, Victory in Europe. On May 8, 1945, the United States cele-
brated V-E Day. "I remember all of us sitting on the street," Christine
Kramer says, "beating tin cans, screaming and hollering. 'Cause we knew
my brother was going to come home."

Most Americans welcomed the news more reservedly—with hymns at
church, with toasts among friends. Although one stage of the war had
finished, "there was another, possibly more difficult, stage coming up,"
Lee Saunders explains. To beat Japan, the United States was planning to
invade the island—an offensive likely to produce a terrible number of
casualties. Just taking the tiny island of Okinawa that spring had killed
almost 7,000 soldiers, sailors, and marines. Tired troops returning from

Europe would be routed through the United States, then out across the Pacific.

But World War II ended more quickly than anyone expected. On August 6, 1945, under orders from President Harry Truman, FDR's successor, the B-29 aircraft *Enola Gay* dropped an atomic bomb with

*The atomic bomb explosion at Nagasaki*

a force equal to 20,000 tons of dynamite on the city of Hiroshima, Japan. If the Japanese "do not now accept our terms," Truman announced, "they may expect a rain of ruin from the air, the like of which has never been seen on this earth.... We have spent two billion dollars on the greatest scientific gamble in history—and won." Three days later, a second atomic bomb devastated Nagasaki.

News of this secret superweapon awed Americans. Most people approved of Truman's decision to use it. Only later, as grisly images of destruction reached the public, did the home front worry about what science had unleashed. In Hiroshima, more than 80,000 people died, some with the pattern of their kimonos burned into their skin. "It felt like we'd bitten into something much bigger than we could possibly handle," Sylvia Choate says. Christine Kramer agrees. "I think it was a fear in everybody."

But when the Japanese surrendered, jubilation overpowered every other emotion. On V-J (Victory in Japan) Day, September 2, Truman declared a two-day holiday, and banks, factories, stores—even the stock exchange—closed. Sylvia Choate went into downtown Boston with friends:

> There was the most incredible party the day the war ended. ... I've never seen such crowds and such shrieking and carrying on. Almost scary crowds.... There were obviously some servicemen around, and people... were exuberant.... There wasn't one speech, there must have been 50 speeches on various corners.

In Salt Lake City, residents snake-danced in the rain. In New York, they shredded phone books into confetti. In San Francisco, they cheered for two young women skinny-dipping in a fountain. At times, the gaiety got out of hand as rowdy bands of GIs near military bases looted liquor stores and harassed women. In New York City, hospitals treated 800 emergencies in the first hours of V-J Day. Even people who stayed home, or attended one of the thousands of church and synagogue services of thanksgiving, could not escape the clamor of horns, whistles, bells, and sirens.

*V-J Day celebrations*

Gas rationing ceased immediately. Soon curfews, blackouts, and other wartime restrictions were eliminated. By November, only sugar was still scarce. Trains, buses, planes, and ships remained jammed, however, with troops on their way home.

## "YOU'D BE SO NICE TO COME HOME TO"

While movies and magazine covers romanticized the returning soldier's first smooch and the happy moment of reunion, the period of transition that followed was often difficult. Veterans needed time to unwind, to make plans, and to get to know children whom they may have seen only in photographs. "Everyone had problems of one kind or the other in adjusting," says Lee Saunders, "psychological problems, financial problems, professional or occupational problems."

Anticipating these problems, Congress had passed the Servicemen's

Readjustment Act in June 1944. Known as the GI Bill, it enabled veterans to borrow money at low rates of interest to buy houses or open businesses. Those who returned to college or studied a trade received free tuition, books, and a monthly stipend. Unemployed veterans could join the "52-20 Club" and collect $20 a week from the government for up to a year. Employers were required by law to rehire those workers who had quit to fight. But the GI Bill gave veterans what they longed for even more: a fresh start.

Despite the promise of opportunities, many servicemen floundered for a spell. Like other young veterans who had shouldered huge responsibilities during the war, Sandy Whitman tried and quit several jobs before settling on a career. "It's difficult to go from commanding officer of anything to the mail room of a corporation," he says.

Disabled veterans, who had been trickling back to stateside Veterans Administration hospitals throughout the war, had to come to terms with their handicaps. About 17,000 servicemen lost arms or legs. Many soldiers also suffered "combat fatigue," with symptoms ranging from nightmares to alcohol abuse to personality changes. "I had a brother-in-law who was in the marines, and he went through H-E-L-L,"

*Veterans headed for discharge crowd a troop train through France.*

The Best Years of Our Lives *portrayed the struggles of returning GIs.*

Christine Kramer says. "Because he was on Iwo Jima and all those places, right on the front line. He left a sweet guy, but when he came back, he was nasty."

While most soldiers denied that the trauma of battle had scarred them, articles in the press warned the folks back home that men might have trouble picking up where they left off. *The Best Years of Our Lives*, a 1946 movie that won eight Academy Awards, dramatized the dilemmas of three vets from Boom City, U.S.A. One is shocked to find his teenage children grown up. Another, a decorated bombardier, doesn't want to return to his dead-end job in a soda shop. The third, a seaman played by a real-life disabled veteran, comes home with hooks instead of hands. The navy has trained him to open doors and light matches, but he has to learn on his own how to accept the love of his girlfriend. Although these men believed they had given their country the best years of their lives, the movie implies that better ones lay ahead.

*These defense plant workers lost their jobs at war's end.*

War had changed women, too. Although some women had been apprehensive at first, most enjoyed their defense jobs. A 1944 survey revealed that 75 to 80 percent of women in defense production wanted to keep working after the war. But the government cancelled contracts with defense plants as soon as the fighting ended. Factories laid off those without seniority, including women and many black workers. New jobs went to veterans and other men.

With no notice, Frankie Cooper lost her seven-day-a-week shipbuilding job in Oregon. She recalled in *The Homefront*:

> It was a great blow. I know the pride I had felt during the war. I just felt ten feet tall. Here I was doing an important job, and doing it well, and then all at once here comes V-J Day... and I'm back making homemade bread.

Returning servicemen were not prepared to find wives who were disappointed with traditional female roles. Many women didn't want to turn over the checkbook, the steering wheel, and the decision-making to their husbands. As Dellie Hahne remarked in *The Homefront*, her husband "had left a shrinking violet and come home to a very strong oak tree. This did not make him very happy." World War II had planted the first seeds of the women's liberation movement that followed in the 1960s and 1970s.

Relationships died and bloomed after V-J Day. In 1946, couples divorced at a record rate. But wedding bells were also ringing steadily throughout the late 1940s. In 1945, a new radio show called "Bride and Groom" featured live ceremonies on the air. BettyLou married Bill Folley and, like millions of other young couples, they started a family, part of the baby boom that lasted until 1964.

The housing shortage continued. "Apartments and houses didn't have vacancies for years," says Lee Saunders. "There were no places for these young couples. They were all doubled up with their in-laws." Sylvia and Sandy Whitman shared an apartment over his mother's garage, and when their second son was born, they renovated a closet as a nursery. She recalls:

> The *World Telegram* ran an article on "VETERANS' HOUSING—CHILDREN PLACED IN CLOSETS." They came and interviewed [us] and saw it. The closet was actually fine; it held a crib, a bureau, and a window.... Tiny, but it was all right.

War had uprooted many Americans, and some couples moved far from their families to make a home of their own. After his discharge, Lee Saunders returned to New York City. He and his bride slept on a couch in his parents' apartment. On a whim, he took advantage of a free audition that the National Broadcasting Company (NBC) gave to any veteran. When a radio station in North Carolina offered him a job as a newscaster, Saunders and his wife set out for the South.

Housing did not catch up with the demand for several years. When the unions struck at Westinghouse after the war, Herman Kramer quit and began building houses on his father's farmland. He recalls:

> You could sell anything you could put together. Of course, you couldn't get any material. You had to build your own doors; you had to build your own windows.... Each room had a different kind of floor. Whatever you could buy, you bought. And whatever you could put up—these servicemen came back, they had to have some place to live.

Soon housing developers teamed with manufacturers to make construction faster and cheaper. By 1949, entrepreneur William Levitt was able to build four-room homes that sold for $7,990—which translated into a monthly mortgage payment of $60. Long Island, New York, was the site of the first "Levittown": street after street of identical houses with outdoor barbecues, washing machines, and built-in TV sets. All across America, the GI couples of the 1940s settled into the suburban life of the 1950s.

A few storm clouds lingered, however. Disappointed by the return to "normalcy"—and bigotry—black Americans, joined by some white liberals, launched the civil rights movement in the 1950s. Free, yet disheartened by life in the relocation camps, some Japanese families struck out from the West for Chicago and the East. But most returned to California, to bankrupt businesses and vandalized homes. Although internees had lost more than $400 million in property, the U.S. government offered only $38 million, less than 10 percent, as compensation. Not until 1988 did Congress issue an official apology and vote $1.25 billion in payments to Japanese American camp survivors.

## "GOD BLESS AMERICA"

The deadline pressure of the war had sharpened American industry, particularly management techniques. Soon companies were churning out appliances, clothes, and cosmetics to satisfy a hungry market. Big business had elbowed out Mom-and-Pop operations during the war, and many never recovered. Small farmers sold their land to corporations. Giant supermarkets replaced corner groceries.

Research and development in the defense industry had led to manufacturing innovations. After the war, TVs and air conditioners became widely available, as did plastics. By the end of the decade, children were playing with new toys such as Silly Putty, a silicone product developed for use in B-29 turbosuperchargers. Herman Kramer remembers:

> Things were moving so fast, you didn't have time to think about anything.... All these new houses were being built and people were buying them, and new cars were being built and people were buying them. And all this work was available.... It was a boom.

*Levittown, Pennsylvania, was one of thousands of postwar subdivision developments built for returning veterans and their families.*

*Celebrating V-J Day in New York City*

Scientists dazzled the public with wartime discoveries. Antibiotics and sulfa drugs cured deadly infections and diseases such as pneumonia. The pesticide DDT killed mosquitoes that carried malaria and insects that ate farm crops. Science was a two-edged sword, though. It turned out that DDT not only destroyed pests but also poisoned birds and animals. Nuclear power promised plentiful energy, but nuclear weapons could destroy the planet. The arms race between the United States and the Soviet Union, which began in the late 1940s, filled people with anxiety.

In 1945 and 1949, at trials closely followed on the home front, the United States and its allies prosecuted war criminals. High-ranking Germans found guilty of ordering the imprisonment and execution of six million European Jews received death sentences. Japanese officers responsible for the mistreatment of prisoners of war were hanged. Generous with its wealth, the United States also helped rebuild battle-torn Europe with the Marshall Plan, a massive package of food and economic aid.

Most Americans believed the United States government was standing up for right in the late 1940s, just as it had during the war. After all the hardships of World War II, people looked forward to peace, progress, and prosperity. In *The Homefront*, Laura Briggs, who moved from an Idaho farm to a California boom town and back again in the 1940s, spoke for a generation:

> I think everyone had more hope.... When the war was over, we felt really good about ourselves. We had saved the world from an evil that was unspeakable.... We were so innocent and naive.... Life was going to be glorious from now on, because we deserved it.

WITHDRAWN
Speedway Public Library

# SELECTED BIBLIOGRAPHY

Bailey, Ronald H. *The Home Front: U.S.A.* New York: Time-Life Books, 1977.

Boardman, Barrington. *Flappers, Bootleggers, "Typhoid Mary," and the Bomb: An Anecdotal History of the United States from 1923-1945.* New York: Harper & Row Publishers, 1988.

Casdorph, Paul D. *Let the Good Times Roll: Life at Home in America during WWII.* New York: Paragon House, 1989.

Duden, Jane. *Timelines 1940s.* New York: Crestwood House, 1989.

Gesensway, Deborah and Mindy Roseman. *Beyond Words: Images from America's Concentration Camps.* Ithaca, New York: Cornell University Press, 1987.

Gordon, Lois and Alan. *American Chronicle: Seven Decades in American Life.* New York: Crown Publishers, Inc., 1987.

Harris, Mark Jonathan, et al. *The Homefront: America during World War II.* New York: G. P. Putnam's Sons, 1984.

Hartmann, Susan M. *American Women in the 1940s: The Home Front and Beyond.* Boston: Twayne Publishers, 1982.

Hoehling, A. A. *Home Front, U.S.A.: The Story of World War II Over Here.* New York: Thomas Y. Crowell Company, 1966.

Honey, Maureen. *Creating Rosie the Riveter: Class, Gender, and Propaganda during World War II.* Amherst: University of Massachusetts Press, 1984.

Hoopes, Roy. *Americans Remember the Home Front.* New York: Hawthorn Books, Inc., 1977.

Hornby, George, ed. *The Great American Scrapbook*. New York: Crown Publishers, Inc., 1985.

Keegan, John. *The Second World War*. New York: Viking, 1990.

Kitano, Harry H.L. *Japanese Americans: The Evolution of a Subculture*. Englewood Cliffs, New Jersey: Prentice-Hall, 1976.

Litoff, Judy Barrett et al. *Miss You: The World War II Letters of Barbara Wooddall Taylor and Charles E. Taylor*. Athens: The University of Georgia Press, 1990.

Perrett, Geoffrey. *Days of Sadness, Years of Triumph: The American People 1939-1945*. New York: Coward, McCann & Geoghegan, Inc. 1973.

Ravitch, Diane, ed. *The American Reader: Words That Moved a Nation*. New York: HarperCollins, 1990.

Satterfield, Archie. *The Home Front—An Oral History of the War Years in America: 1941-1945*. N.p.: Playboy Press, 1981.

Terkel, Studs. *"The Good War": An Oral History of World War Two*. New York: Ballantine Books, 1984.

# INDEX

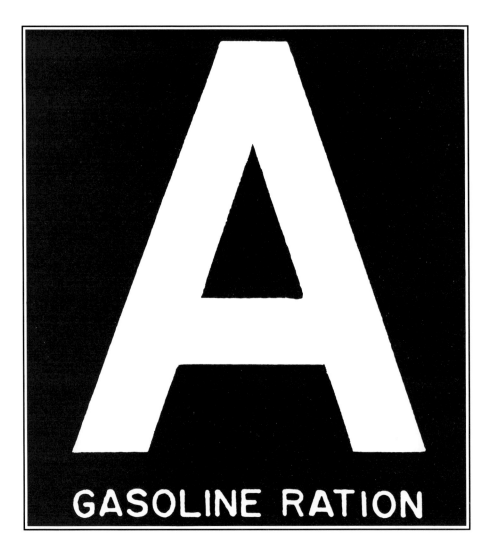

## ACKNOWLEDGMENTS

Photographs reproduced with permission of: National Archives, pp. 2, 6, 7, 8, 10 (top and bottom), 14, 15, 16, 18, 22, 25, 32 (left), 33, 37, 40, 47, 51, 53, 56, 62, 64, 65, 67 (both), 68, 70, 74; George C. Marshall Research Library, pp. 13, 26, 28, 32 (right), 80; The Bettman Archive, pp. 19, 34, 43, 45 (bottom), 48, 52, 60, 73; Chicago Public Library, Special Collections Division, pp. 21, 41; Minneapolis Public Library and Information Center, p. 24; Swarthmore College Peace Collection, p. 29; Minnesota Historical Society, pp. 30, 45 (top), 55; Kansas State Historical Society, pp. 38 (top and bottom), 42; Hollywood Book and Poster, pp. 58, 69.

Front cover: Minneapolis Public Library and Information Center; back cover: George C. Marshall Research Library.